A GUIDE TO BUDDHIST TEMPLES

A GUIDE
TO
BUDDHIST TEMPLES

F. F. MARTINUS

GYAN

Published by

Gyan Publishing House
5, Ansari Road
Daryaganj, New Delhi-110002
Phone: 011-47034999, 9811692060
E-mail: books@gyanbooks.com

Distribution Network
gyanbooks.com
India, USA, Canada, UK, Australia, France

ISBN : 978-81-212-3441-2 (PB)
First Published, Madras, 1907

2nd Impression 2020

Printed at: Gyan Press, Delhi.

A GUIDE

TO

BUDDHIST TEMPLES,

BY

F. F. MARTINUS,

Sub-Editor, "Morning Times".

COLOMBO:

THE "CEYLON EXAMINER" PRESS.

1907.

DEDICATED

BY SPECIAL PERMISSION

TO

T. E. SIR HENRY BLAKE, G. C. M. G., GOVERNOR OF CEYLON,

AND

LADY EDITH BLAKE.

PREFACE.

The scope of this book is to provide the visitor to Colombo with a guide-book to Buddhist Temples in general, and to the Temple of the Prince Priest in particular.

The reason for the choice of the latter is that it is one of the largest temples in Colombo, and has the largest images; it provides the most sights; and has a very effective guide in the courteous Incumbent.

F. F. M.

COLOMBO, *31st May, 1907.*

INTRODUCTION.

Whatever may be thought of the statement of it here, from a Buddhist point of view the fact is undeniable that to a tourist one of the chief sights in Colombo is a Buddhist temple. There are many good reasons why this should be so. Even if the plea of novelty and newness—for there is nothing even remotely resembling a Buddhist temple in Europe, America, or Australia—be put by as too apparent for mention, there yet remains the good reason that in Ceylon is found the most primitive form of Buddhism; and if Buddhism is to be seen in its best and most favourable aspects, it is in Ceylon. That reason will, however, only appeal to a limited number; but all visitors to these shores can be assured of a good half hour of the most novel and pleasing interest in a temple. They will see there what is entirely outside the run of sights and shows at the various ports of this highway of the sea; and they will have gained a nearer and more accurate estimate of the true Oriental than any rushing through the business parts of the town, where the impressions are, to a large extent, such as to be got at any port east of the Suez. Here in a temple everything is new—the yellow-robed Buddhist mendicant, with his shaven poll and his meditative eyes; the quaint temple, and the large collection there of images and frescoes instinct with an ancient and forgotten art; the seductive, fugitive, but very pleasant, odour of spices and resin incense in the image house and the sacred libraries,—the latter full of quaint rectangular block books of palmyra leaves threaded by a coloured string; the umbrageous bo-tree, the sacred tree of the Buddhists, with the polyglot of offerings and quaint hand-lamps round its masonry basement, etc. The list of attractions can be interminably extended, but these are experiences never to be got anywhere else. Set the several sights in their native setting, with the various peoples of the country in their picturesque costume, the flower-sellers, the betel-nut vendors, and the other usual concomitants to a temple, and a series of pictures will have been gained which will be a lingering memory of a very crowded and pleasantly spent half hour.

There is a certain amount of sameness in the temples in the maritime provinces—so that to those having no particular object (each temple has its peculiarities and specialities) a visit to one will be all that need be undertaken—a great advantage when the exigencies of a visitor's time are taken into account. That being so, it is all important to visit the temple which is the completest of its kind and has the largest number of attractions, and has the most interesting information to offer. The visitor will be well advised to go to the Dipaduttamarama, in Kotahena, commonly known as the Prince Priest's Temple. It takes no more than fifteen minutes to drive to it from the jetty, the route being through the busiest part of the city, and thus having its own recommendations. The Temple is quite close to St. Lucia's (the Roman Catholic) Cathedral, the largest Church in the Island, to the Anglican Cathedral, the Dock Works, etc. It is the temple that is most often visited by tourists. His Excellency Sir Henry Blake (Governor of Ceylon), and Lady Blake, and, when she was in the Island, H. R. H. Princess Louise of Schleswig-Holstein, and nearly all distinguished visitors to the Island have visited the Temple more than once. The prominent notabilities, among them the Duchess of St. Albans, H.I.H. Prince Tsai, Imperial High Commissioner, who have called are too numerous to mention. Their autographs will be found in the visitors' book of the Temple and of its sacred museum. At this Temple, too, the visitor will have a most engaging and interesting guide—the only Oriental Buddhist monk with an English education in all Asia, and a Prince of the Royal House of Siam, H.R.H. P.C. Jinavaravansa Thero (the late Prince Prisdang) C.M.G., A. M. I. C. E., etc., commonly known as the Prince Priest. His kindness in acting as guide is invaluable, and the visitor will have every opportunity to take an intelligent interest in what he sees. There is much that will require explanation to be thoroughly appreciated, and the Prince Priest makes it his business to give every assistance. The images, the frescoes and ancient paintings, the bas reliefs, the depictions of mythology,—all have their peculiar interest and charm; and with the Prince Priest for guide these charms become possible. This Temple again is the only temple with a labyrinth, and here too is a sacred museum, the only one of its kind, and replete with rare and unique relics, ancient sculptures, images, plaster-casts, ancient manuscripts, historical relics, and exhibits not to be seen anywhere else in Ceylon. The claims of this Temple to its popularity with tourists do not end here, but in a general survey nothing more need be said. The following pages will deal more in detail with the chief centres of interest

I.

THE KOTAHENA TEMPLE.

THE LARGEST IMAGE HOUSE IN COLOMBO.

The Dipaduttamarama Temple at Kotahena, or more commonly known as the Temple of the Prince Priest, for the Prince Priest is the Incumbent thereof, was built in 1860, and considerably improved by its late incumbent Migetuwatte priest, who was widely known for his rhetorical powers and capabilities as a controversialist in Ceylon. The great Buddhist revival is due partly to his public addresses and activities; and he is directly responsible for winning for Ceylon the large-hearted sympathy and the unstinted labours of the late Colonel Olcott at the dawn of the Theosophical movement. Owing to the great popularity of this priest this Temple grew in elaboration and size, till today it is the largest modern temple in Ceylon, and is regularly visited by pilgrims and travellers.

In structure the temple is modern. There is practically nothing to suggest old Sinhalese architecture—a result of the foreign influence in the maritime provinces of Ceylon, and the apathy and decadence into which Buddhism had fallen before the great Buddhist revival of two decades ago. But though deprived of all suggestions of the ancient style of Sinhalese architecture, the Temple is not without its peculiar formation and arrangement, which is largely followed by all modern temples in the maritime districts.

Entering the Temple by the side door the visitor steps on to a corridor, or verandah, which runs round the three sides of the Temple; and before him are rich Oriental decorations, painted figures and frescoes of a striking kind. These decorations are typically Sinhalese, and common to all Buddhist temples in the country. They have been copied from an ancient temple in the interior of Ceylon.

This entrance is immediately in front of the

Middle Door,

and the arch over this door-way is formed of the depiction of a mythical sea-monster known as Makara. The paintings and frescoes round the door call for special notice. The gods Siva and Brahma stand on the right and left respectively, with the figures of the Doratupala, the guardian god of the door, standing by their side. The painting just over the door represents a miracle said to have occurred at the Shwe Dagon, at Rangoon; but the details of the occurrence have been lost.

On the wall to the right of this door come, in order, fresco figures of Siriyakantava, wife of Vishnu; a statue of Somante Deva, tutelary god of Adam's Peak; and a fresco of Sarasti, wife of Maha Brahma.

To the left of this door, on the wall, are a fresco of Irandati, wife of Punnaka, sub-chief of the Yakkhos; a large statue of Bandara Devata, an incarnation, according to a late Sinhalese legend, of a Kandyan chief of Alutnuwara and Bambarku, on account of his virtues; and another fresco of Punnaka, the Yakkho chieftain.

These paintings extend on either side to the groups round the

Doors to the Right and Left

of this middle door, and these again claim attention.

Over the archway of the door to the right come the King of the Nagas and the King of the Yakkhos, the two aboriginal races of Ceylon. These are on the left and right respectively, and are, by name, Virupakkha, the guardian god of the western quarter, and Vesavanno, guardian god of the northern quarter. The two outside figures, next the two kings, are those of the Doratupala Deviyo, the guardian god of the door. The fresco group round the door illustrates one stage of the life of the Buddha. This particular statue represents the Mitriya Bodhisatwa, an incarnation of the Buddha, with his attendants in the Brahma world. The two small figures over the arch are those of ascetics, and the last figure, quite at the corner, is again the guardian of the door.

The decorations round the door to the left of the middle door are similar in arrangement. The figures over the arch are those of the King of the Gandhabbas and the King of the Kumbhrandas. These are the left and right figures respectively, and are, to give the full designation, Thataratta, guardian god of the eastern quarter and tutelary god of music, and Virudha, guardian god of the southern quarter. Outside these figures come the familiar figure of Doratupala, the guardian of the door. Over the archway are two small figures representing the Vidyadharas, the tutelary gods of charms or of the sciences.

The Nirwana Chapel.

The visitor so far will have viewed merely the outside of the Temple—the paintings on the walls and round the doorways. Returning to the middle door, he will, by it, gain admittance to the Nirvana Chapel, so called from the principal statue there depicting the Buddha in the posture of passing away, "in which nothing whatever is left behind", to create a being after him out of his *samkhara*—his thought forms, motives, merits, demerits, etc. The Master has already said his last words to his Bhikku (monk) following, and given his last exhortation: "Behold now, brethren, I exhort you. Decay is inherent in all component things. Work out your salvation with diligence!"

The expression on the face of this statue and the posture of the body both express calm and peacefulness; the mind ruffled by no considerations of the world, by no affections, and no passions. The shield at the back of the head represents the aura of six colours—colours which are very familiar on banners and flags at all Buddhistic decorations.

To this statue the faithful draw near with flowers and lamps and candles and incense and money, as pious offerings, on the holy days, the days of the four phases of the moon; and these same devout stream into this chamber by the hundreds, from early morning till a late hour in the night, bringing their offerings, which overflow the tables meant to receive them and scatter themselves all over the floor. Lights and sweet scents and incense smoke fill the chamber, with the unending tale of these offerings.

The scene here is specially striking on the nights when special addresses are delivered, or when one of the devout, in his efforts to do some meritorious deed, decorates the temple precincts with bunting and the tender leaf of the cocoanut palm and with Chinese paper lanterns.

This recumbent statue is the largest in the Colombo district, and measures 42 ft.

To the left of it is a figure of the Metteya Boddhisatwa. This represents the future Buddha in the Tusita Brahma Loka (the Buddhist highest heaven). He will then be born again, for the last time, on earth, and when he appears he will be the *Metteya Buddha*, the fifth and last Buddha of the present world cycle. Then will be the Buddhist millenium, of peace on earth and good-will towards all men, as this "metteyya", "loving kindness", indicates.

Near this statue is a large brass chandelabra, of exquisite Sinhalese workmanship, and one very generally admired.

In this room, too, are interesting frescoes claiming attention. On the front wall are the guardian gods of the four quarters of the globe (already referred to, page 8) and on an adjoining wall, to the left of the door by which the visitor will leave the chamber, is a fresco of Sakka or Indra, chief of the gods of the Tavatimsa heaven.

On the upper part of the walls are portrait paintings of the eighty Asiti Mahasevakas, or the Great Disciples of the Buddha, and the whole ceiling is covered with fresco work of Sinhalese style—a very fine example of an art now dying out in Ceylon.

THE FIGURE OF VISHNU.

One other statue remains in this Nirvana Chapel to be noted before passing out of this chamber. It stands by itself, in a glass case, and is the figure of Vishnu, the Hindu deity. This statue rivals the statue of the recumbent Buddha in the amount of offerings it receives. Hindus and Buddhists alike come to it, and their faith is that Vishnu offers greater promise of worldly blessings, inasmuch as he can be prayed to, and by means of offerings propitiated and made merciful.

The presence of this Hindu god, enshrined in a Buddhist temple, is seemingly incongruous until it is remembered that, according to the political history of the Island, the two religions overlapped, and were, to a large extent, lost the one in the other. The incongruity may also be accounted for by the fact that though in theory the Ceylon form of Buddhism is the purest, in practice it is not so.

IN THE GALLERY.

Stepping out of the Nirwana Chapel, the visitor regains the gallery, or verandah, and to his left, at the extreme end of the passage, are two statues, of only passing interest, meant to represent King Suddhodana and his consort, Maya Devi, the parents of Gautama Buddha.

On the wall he is a curious picture, by a Burmese artist, depicting the *Mara yuddha*—the contest with the

GALLERY OF THE KOTAHENA TEMPLE

A CUPBOARD IN THE ROOM OF THE RENUNCIATION.

powers of darkness. It is to represent the purification of the mind by meditation, and shows the process by which the Buddha's mind was purged under the bo tree. The evil tendencies are represented in physical forms tormenting him.

In this same gallery is a long, glass case, in which are 24 statues, representing the Buddhas of the previous *kalpas*, or world cycles. To these Buddhas Gautama Buddha vowed that he would himself become a Buddha. Brief accounts of these 24 Buddhas are found in the Buddhist scriptures, and the figures themselves are familiar in Buddhist temples. The names of the 24 appear on the statues.

In this gallery, too, is a fresco, in four parts, illustrating the well-known "birth stories" of the Kusa Jatakas. All around are illuminated pictures, of Siamese origin, showing the Buddha on several important occasions in his life.

Here, again, are kept the national flags of the various Buddhist countries, manufactured, for decorative purposes, by the Prince Priest.

The Burmese Chapel.

From the gallery a doorway leads into the Burmese Chapel, so named from the circumstance that the decorations here are by Burmese artists, and the image is one offered by Burmese pilgrims. Over the doorway is the fresco representing the birth story from the Vesantara Jataka, the last but one birth of the Buddha as the Boddhisatwa, and in which he perfected one of the ten qualifications (*paramitha*) requisite for attaining Buddhahood—the perfection of charity. According to this birth story Vesantara Rajah gave away his very wife and children in secret of this perfection.

On the lower portion of the wall at this door is the illustration of another "birth story", from the Sarsaka Jataka, which, incidentally, shows the origin of the popular belief in Ceylon, and the Orient generally, of the hare in the moon.

The difference in the style of the decorative art in this Burmese chamber will be at once noticed. The paintings on the walls, the carving of the shrine, as well as of the recumbent statue in the glass case, are of a distinct type, and differ widely from the Sinhalese.

The statue is of alabaster. It was made in Burma, and represents the Buddha resting on his right side—with the right foot over the left, "in the manner of a lion". The

Buddha here is "resting conscious and mindful", for a Buddha does not sleep like ordinary mortals "unconsciously, with wandering mind, which also brings dreams". "He has an absence of ideas and thoughts, which are the disturbing element in one's sleep, and his sleep is just peaceful rest."

At the right corner of the front wall of this chapel is a painting representing the birth of the Buddha under a *sala* tree, attended by the Maha Brahma and the goddesses; and the upper part of the wall has the painting of his 80 great disciples at meal time.

In a cupboard in a corner of this room are kept some interesting books on Buddhism, Buddhist pictures, photographs, etc., for sale, in aid of the charity schools of the Temple. Among the photographs is an interesting snapshot of the "ordination" of two Europeans by a European Buddhist priest, in the islet off the Southern Province, "Chulla Lanka", the retreat of the Prince Priest, in 1906—a beautiful little islet, visited by H. E. Sir Henry and Lady Blake, and H. H. Princess Louise of Schleswig-Holstein, and other distinguished visitors.

II.

THE PRINCE PRIEST.

P. C. Jinavaravansa Thero.

In referring to the Temple reference must be made to the present guiding genius of it, the Prince Priest. Since the days of Migetuwatte the temple fell on evil times. Its belongings were spirited away, and the various buildings allowed to fall into disrepair, and subsequently to go into ruins. A new era was inaugurated with the appointment of the Prince Priest as incumbent, and the Temple within it in three brief years is what it is today, owing to the self-denying labours and the whole-hearted devotion of the Prince Priest. He has brought order where chaos reigned; he has undertaken and executed extensive repairs; expelled interlopers from Temple precincts; and has regained to the Temple the ownership of a school-building just outside its gates. The Temple, and the Buddhists in general, have much to be grateful for to him; and in a book of this nature none too conspicuous a place can be given him.

THE PRINCE PRIEST: BEFORE HIS RENUNCIATION.

THE PRINCE PRIEST: IN DEEP MEDITATION.

Small of stature, keen-eyed, always busy, and oftener than not engaged in some trying bit of manual labour, keenly alive to the wants of the Buddhists and how those wants are to be achieved,—the Prince Priest is the most valuable asset progressive Buddhists of Ceylon can have. A casual acquaintance is enough to show how thoroughly and completely he foreswore the privileges of his princely rank when he assumed the yellow robe of the mendicant. The renunciation is stupendous, for a Buddhist priest in Ceylon occupies a very insignificant place today, the influence he once wielded being lost in numbers of ignorant and criminal folk just now in the order. The story of this modern renunciation remains still to be adequately told, but a painfully realistic memorial of it is in the sacred museum of the temple, where a room is set apart for the multiplicity of badges, decorations, insignias, and uniforms, which so well became the Prince that was—

H. R. H. The Prince

Prisdang Choomang of Siam. But this renunciation is not fully, and there is no immediate call for it either, when as a gentleman and a man of culture the Prince Priest is received and held in the highest respect outside the pale of Buddhism by all sections of the community, from the highest in the land downwards. He is a direct descendant of the third King of Siam, and the youngest son of the late H. R. H. Pheachou Rajavaravansa Thieur Krama Khun Râjasinha, the Royal Architect, head of the Department of the Ten Crafts of Siam. He was born on February 23rd, 1852, at the Old Palace of his grandsire, H. M. Ramadhibodi III., at Bangkok.

Early Affliction.

When he was 18 he lost his father, and two years later he was sent, by the present King, to England, to complete his education. He entered King's College, London, in the Applied Science and Art Department, to qualify as a Civil Engineer, and, after a brilliant career, graduated with honours. He won the London Society of Arts' Silver Medal for engineering and architecture, and was elected an Associate Member of the Institute of Civil Engineers. After a trip home for some months he returned to England, to gain a practical experience in engineering under the late Sir John Hankshaw, and to study the working of the Royal Mint, London, and also to acquire some information of the employment of torpedoes for coast defences. Several literary honours also were conferred on him during his stay, among them Associate of King's College, London; Member of the Archæological Society of Portugal; Member of the Oriental Society of France, the Royal Asiatic Society of Great Britain, &c.

His clear and bright intellect and his varied abilities won him a place in

The Diplomatic Service

of Siam. In 1879 he held his first appointment as Interpreter to the Siamese Mission to England and Germany, when also he was decorated by the Emperor of Germany and his own Sovereign. Next he was appointed Second Secretary and Interpreter to the Siamese Special Embassy to present the Grand Cordon of the Most Exalted Order of the White Elephant of Siam to H. M. Queen Victoria, President Grevy of France, the Prince of Wales (the Present King of England), and Frederick (then Crown Prince of Germany), and also to effect certain treaty revisions with the Great Powers. The Siamese Foreign Minister was the Ambassador on this occasion, and Prince Prisdang, the subject of this notice, was then decorated by Queen Victoria, the Emperor of Germany, and the President of France. The King of Siam made him Grand Officer of the Crown of Siam and Colonel of the Vanguard. Subsequently he was appointed Special Envoy Extraordinary to Berlin and Vienna, and conveyed wedding presents from the Siamese Court to the Crown Prince of Austria and Prince William (the present Emperor of Germany). Subsequently he was installed in the high office of Envoy Extraordinary and Minister Plenipotentiary to the Courts of St. James, Berlin, Vienna, the Quirinal, Madrid, Lisbon, Copenhagen, Stockholm, the Hague, Brussels, and to the French and American Republics, and was the first resident representative appointed to foreign courts by Siam. His headquarters were in London first; and when he found his duties in connection with twelve Courts too arduous, he removed to Paris, where he

Founded a Legation.

During this period he performed notable service to his country, among which the conclusion of a convention for regulating the spirit traffic with England, France, and all the rest of the Treaty Powers, a task which several attempts previously made, from the time of the late King of Siam, who sent a special Embassy, had failed to effect.

This unexpected success in his diplomatic career makes him a distinguished public servant in his country in modern times. He was invested by the Siamese King with the higher princely rank the Grand Cross of the Order of the Crown of Siam and Commander of the Family Order of the Chula Chom Kloa. These distinctions were brought to London by royal commission. A royal proclamation was issued, setting forth his services in the most flattering terms, conferring rights and emoluments appertaining to the title. He was, however, not allowed long to continue his diplomatic career in which he had rendered such signal service. On his return to Siam in 1896 he was appointed to the head of the Post and Telegraph Department. He was sent on a complimentary mission to Japan in 1890 with the youngest brother of the King, on which occasion H. I. M. the Emperor of Japan conferred on him the Grand Cross of the Most Distinguished Order of the Rising Sun. The first Japanese Natural Exhibition was opened that year, which the Prince saw. The vast progress which the Japanese have made in all branches of sciences and industry, which the exhibits bear witness, such as would be hard to distinguish between European and Japanese make of everything exhibited, and the almost perfect machinery of Government, the good qualities seen in every Japanese which go to make a great people, seem to have effected him so much that he seemed to have decided not to return to his country. Having resigned his post into the hands of his cousin, the King's brother, on the return of the mission to Hong Kong, giving him his reason in writing his desire not to return to his country for a time, he did not go home with the King's brother. This was the Prince's first sacrifice. It seems that the life, such as it was, had no charms for him. Little by little the desire for a separation from the world forced itself upon his mind, till it became the settled purpose of life. He came over to Ceylon in 1896, and was admitted into the Buddhist brotherhood under the well-known High-Priest to Western Scholars, the Venerable Subhuti Mahathero, on which occasion he made public renunciation of worldly life and possession, and offered all his insignias, decorations, &c., to the shrine of Buddha, which are preserved in the sacred museum at his Temple.

He went later on a pilgrimage to India, and was then appointed Incumbent of the Kotahena Temple, to which he has been a second founder. It was fortunate he came there at the time he did, for the Temple buildings were falling into disrepair, and the successive monsoon rains told the tale of ruins. The buildings were coming down on all hands, and the grounds became the common grounds to the vicinity, where the hangers on at street corners and quarrelsome women came and wrangled, to the disgust of everybody and the despair of all the better class of residents there. The more secluded parts of the grounds, behind the Temple buildings, have seen every type of pollution ; and not even the Municipal Council authorities could regulate the insanitary state of the place. Further and more formidable work there was too, for the 'cuter and sharper Buddhists were on the look out to annex for themselves Temple property. One building, the School-Room just outside the gate of the Temple, was so annexed, and was not regained till after considerable trouble had been spent on it.

THE KOTAHENA TEMPLE.

The Prince Priest set to rectifying all these defects. He appealed for help, and oftener than not it came from the Christian and Hindu communities, the Buddhists being slow to help. The Temple buildings were gradually repaired and brought to the excellent condition in which they now are. The grounds were cleared of the vagrants who congregated there, and those who made Temple land the dumping ground for all their filth were strenuously fought against and expelled. These reforms were not acquiesced in quietly by those with vested interests in the neighbourhood, and base calumny and lying slander against the Prince Priest was particularly active. Nothing was too hard to say against him at the time, but he lived through it. His efforts at regaining the school-room from the lay people, who were making it their private property, led to a mass meeting of the riff-raff, held within the Temple grounds. The Prince Priest was helpless. The Police could not aid him, and the speeches from the platform all breathed threatenings and hate against the Incumbent. But he outlived it. He regained for the Temple the Temple pro-property, and established a free girls' school in that building in addition to the boys' school, which he opened within the premises of the Temple in the second year of his incumbency.

One of the most important works he inaugurated was

FREE TEMPLE-EDUCATION.

In historical times the Buddhist temples were the seminaries and schools of the laity, and at the Kotahena Temple is a special building for the housing of the students. But as temple schools went out of fashion, the *dharmasalas* everywhere remained untenanted, till the purpose of their existence became a mystery. The Prince Priest started a school here. It sought to be a model, with the rest of the Temple, of the temple and grounds contemplated by the Buddhist Temporalities Ordinance, and the experiment, with a keen, cultured enthusiast to work it effectively, was closely watched by everybody who understood the aims of the Incumbent. The school was frequently visited by Sir Henry and Lady Blake, and the authorities of the Public Instruction Office. Elementary education is provided, and the school caters for a sect of the poorest among the community who are outside the pale of every other educational scheme. It is not meant for the Buddhists exclusively. It is a non-sectarian free school, and as such is making its way along slowly but surely. Payment of teachers has been from voluntary donations and gifts from visitors to the Temple grounds, who, as an indication of the pleasure they had derived, contribute their mite into a till specially kept for that purpose.

OUTSIDE THE SCHOOL,

this *dharmasala*, are two travellers' palms, the one named "Father Henry" and the other "Mother Edith". These are memorial trees, planted by Sir Henry Blake and Lady Blake, when they visited the school, and helped to emphasize the working of so desirable a scheme of education and make it better known. [We call the attention of the reader to the Appendix containing the interesting addresses of the Prince Priest to H. E. the Governor on his first visit to the Temple, giving his views on temple education; and to H. E. Lady Blake, on the opening of the girls' free school, also of the Temple. It will repay perusal.]

Besides these again the Prince Priest is entirely responsible for the Sacred Museum within the Temple grounds —the greatest attraction of any Oriental institution in Ceylon. The exhibits are of his collection, and represent the labours of several pilgrimages. He also devotes much of his time to aiding those who seek his counsel and advice in matters of Buddhistical studies and philosophy, and is always ready to discuss and afford information to all who seek it.

III.

THE TEMPLE'S GREATEST ASSET.

THE SACRED MUSEUM.

A particularly interesting part of the Temple is the Sacred Museum, in a building put up for itself. It owes its existence to the Prince Priest, and the exhibits there are of his collection The exhibits are varied, and are such as are not to be seen anywhere else in Ceylon.

A short stair-case brings the visitor to the upper floor, and on the outer verandah, suspended on the walls, are a large collection of plaster casts. A goodly number are those of the oldest sculptures known to Oriental scholars, and known as the Buddhist Railings. The originals are at the great Temple at Buddha Gaya, in India, built by the side of the bo-tree under which the Buddha became "enlightened". They represent scenes of the "Birth stories". Some ot the casts represent monuments and public buildings, and mythological animals. The originals of these casts date at least three centuries before the Christian era. Here also are casts of the lotus flower, a complete set of the various ways it was represented by Buddhist sculptors. The originals of these are at the Chankama, the cloister near the great Temple at Buddha Gaya, set apart as the cloister for walking in meditation. The lotuses are believed to have come up to mark each footstep of the Buddha as he walked in meditation there, and support his feet at every step.

Here, in this outer verandah, is also the cast of a centor, among the medalions, and shows numerous examples of ancient head-dresses. The pair of foot-prints, somewhat modern, is also a cast from the Buddha Gaya, and represents the characteristic marks, as it is supposed, of the feet of great men like the Buddha.

An interesting object in this collection is a cast representing the Sun God, driving in what looks like a Roman chariot. It is from the same Buddhist Railings.

Another exhibit is a big half mask, a cast from the ancient stone statue of Buddha at the ruined city of Auuradhapura (Ceylon), in the Maha Vihara, the temple where a branch of the original sacred bo tree—the tree at Buddha Gaya under which Buddha became enlightened—was planted when Buddhism was first introduced into Ceylon. That was in the third century before Christ. That tree is still standing in Anuradhapura, and is the oldest historically known tree in the world.

At the end of this passage is a large frame, the photographs in it being one of H R.H. Princess Louise Augusta of Schleswig-Holstein, with her autograph, and prints of the snap-shots taken by her at Chulla Lanka, the Prince Priest's islet of retreat on the southern coast of Ceylon. The Princess visited this islet when she accompanied Their Excellencies the Governor and Lady Blake, who held a reception to the Buddhists of Matara at this place, on their first visit to the south. The photographs were presented by the Princess to the Prince Priest as mementos of the visit.

Immediately below this picture frame is a show-case with some of the precious treasures in the museum, and, besides other exhibits, is one of the only three ancient bronze statues of Buddha ever discovered in India. A description of these bronzes is given in the journals of the Royal Asiatic Society of London. Another exhibit here is an exact impression of the famous tooth relic of Kandy, taken on sandalwood paste and cast in plaster-of-Paris.

The various exhibits in this show-case are carefully labelled, so that there is no necessity to give any further particulars of them here.

The Main Apartment.

So far the visitor will have been on the outer verandah. On entering the main apartment, the visitor will see before him a book-case, containing sacred ola books with gilded letters. These are the books used in Burmah for the ordination of priests. There is in the case also the oldest palm-leaf manuscript in existence in Ceylon, namely Buddhaghosa's *Visuddhimagga*. The various books are described in the case, and the visitor will find no difficulty in distinguishing them.

Opposite this case are curious musical instruments, of bamboo work, and familiar to visitors to Burmah and Siam. The instruments consist of a wooden boat-like frame work, and strips of bamboo are threaded into two strings spanning the frame work from end to end. These strips are tuned and toned and graduated into a chromatic scale, and when struck with a cotton-headed stick emit very sweet and musical sounds.

Relic Room.

At one end of this main appartment, to the right, is a little room, the chief object here being a relic of the sacred bo tree under which the Enlightenment took place. It is the oldest relic known to the Buddhist world. The whole tree was found dead, and buried in a specially built vault at Buddha Gaya, and was discovered by the late General Cunningham, Archæological Commissioner, when the great temple of Buddha Gaya was restored by the Government of India in 1886. The relic in this museum was obtained by the Prince Priest from the Museum at Calcutta, whither the few remaining bits of the decaying wood had been removed when the discovery took place.

In this room, also, is another interesting relic, a tiny, but authentic, piece of the begging bowl of Buddha, a few pieces of which were discovered in a huge monument near Bombay known as the Sopara Stupa.

Another relic in this room is a strip of the inscribed Asoka column, which marked the very spot at which the Buddha was born. It was in the Nepaul Terrai, in the village known as Negliva. This relic was obtained by the Prince Priest on his pilgrimage to the place in 1898.

The "Unique Statue"

In a like room at the opposite end of the main apartment is a faithful copy of a most wonderful bit of sculpture, the only one of its kind in all India. It represents the Buddha before he attained to the enlightened state, practising the severe penance which, according to Hindu belief of the time, was the only means of knowing the true purposes of life. The original of this cast is at the Lahore Museum, and was found in the Swat Valley, in the north of the Punjab. It is interesting to note the classical style of the Greeks in this statue. The mind will recall the invasion of India by Alexander the Great, and of the efforts of Seleucus Nikator, then in the height of his glory, to rival his master's success in the north by an invasion southward. The small kingdoms were consolidated by Chandragupta into the one organised Empire of Magadha, and Seleucus assailed it in vain. He had to cede all his provinces west of the Indus to the conquerors, and gave the hand of his

THE "UNIQUE STATUE" OF BUDDHA.

PRINCE PRISDANG OF SIAM.

daughter in marriage to the victorious Emperor of all India. Possibly some of Seleucus' Greek followers settled down and embraced the religion of the country and took to stone-carving, of which this statue is not the only lingering remnant. The statue at least indicates the influence of Greek art in the country, and all the sculptures found in the extensive ruins in the Swat Valley show marked evidences of the Grecian style. This statue is known as the "Unique Statue", from the fact of its being the only one of its kind found in India. It is at least 2,200 years old, belonging to the fourth century before Christ.

In the same room as this "Unique Statue" is a carved stone depicting Maya Devi, the Queen Consort of King Suddhodana, lying on a bed. The stone refers to a widely known incident in her life. It was on a full-moon night, and she, according to custom, was keeping the ten precepts as an Upasika. She then dreamt of a white elephant which came down from the sky and entered her womb. From this dream it was that court astrologers foretold that if he who was then conceived did not attain to Buddhahood he would become a Universal Emperor. She was from that day regarded as a holy woman, and seven days after giving birth to her child, who afterwards became the Buddha, she passed away and was reborn in the Tavatinisa heaven as a goddess.

The Story of a Renunciation.

In this same museum building is a room to the back of the main apartment, and may fitly be styled the "Room of a modern Renunciation". It relates, in mute accents, the story of the Siamese Prince giving up his earthly greatness to the unpromising, unattractive life of an ascetic and recluse. Here are the various decorations, medals, uniforms, diplomas, etc., which were so intimately associated with the life of Prince Prisdang, C. M. G., of Siam. They are all in glass cases, and they preach the hard ethical principle of the absolute necessity of renunciation and unattachment to become free from worldly care, from the "pomps and vanities of this wicked world", as a preliminary step to becoming a member of the Holy Order of the Sangha, as a Sakiyaputto. The Prince joined the Order in this country in 1896, in the Society of the Amarapura Sect, one of the two great "lines of pupilary succession of the Buddhist Priesthood", introduced into Ceylon from Burma in 1802.

The Magic Mirror.

In this Room of the Renunciation is a very rare exhibit —the wonderful Japanese metal mirror. In shape it is not very different from an ordinary hand mirror, but it is entirely of metal. It has a highly polished smooth surface on which there is not the slightest indication of a dent or any suggestion of lines. But the moment the mirror is held to the lights of a lamp or the rays of the sun, and the reflection allowed to fall on a wall or on a screen, there is a perfect representation of the Buddha in a standing posture: It is justly called the *magic* mirror, for it is nothing less than magic. The art of its manufacture is now lost; and though a few are met with in Japan, they are jealously guarded, lest they escape out of the country. They are said to be of a fabulous age, over 3,000 years old. It is regarded as a treasure in Japan, and priceless in value. There is a mirror of the kind in the Royal Temple in Siam; and besides this and the one in the Colombo Sacred Museum, there are none in the East outside Japan.

Library.

On the ground floor of the Sacred Museum is a visitors' room and the sacred library. The room has been the home of several Europeans who sought the quiet of the place and the advantages of the library to study with the intention of joining the Buddhist priesthood. The befriending of these earnest students has been no inconsiderable work of the Siam Prince, and his assistance as a guide and tutor will be gratefully acknowledged by several who have since joined the arduous role of the yellow-robed monk. Several of these young men have, after a course of hard study, passed to Chulla Lanka, an islet off the south coast of Ceylon—a retreat presented to the Prince Priest, and laid out by him with caves and primitive dwellings of the kind—where they put in a period of meditation in complete isolation from the outside world.

In the library, occupying a whole wall, is a framed board on which are samples of architectural and engineering models. This was put together by the Ceylon Technical College for the St. Louis World's Exposition, and on its return was presented to the Temple School, to help the pupils in the manual and industrial training which is to be there imparted.

The Library was also the recipient of the Pali Text Society's publications from the Government of Ceylon, which buy a number of copies for the purpose of encouraging the study of Oriental literature.

THE DHARMASALA.

The building to the right of the image house is a large block where the monks live. The forepart of it, a large, open hall, is the *Dharmasala*. Such a hall is found in almost all temples; and in historic times, when the temples were the only seats of learning, these *Dharmasalas* were crowded with pupils.

The buildings were built from the munificence of the laity of that day. With the spread of education, and the gradual usurpation of the laity in the work of teaching, these *Dharmasalas* came to be untenanted. The effort to start a school in this particular *Dharmasala* was due to the desire to regain for the Temple its ancient right of being the centre of education. The Boys' School in the *Dharmasala* is a non-sectarian free school. It is as open to Christian and Hindu as to Buddhist; but this in no way infringes the donor's expectations in making the offering of the *Dharmasala* to the Temple, as Buddhist charity, from its very nature, has to be unconditional. It has to be "charity for charity's sake". Under the circumstances the Kotahena *Dharmasala* is free to teach Buddhists as it is to teach Christians or children of any other religion.

The boys' school was started in 1902 and was soon found to cater for a class of the community who were generally neglected. There was a large class of the poorest in the town which were outside the pale of all educational schemes, and these took care that there was no dearth of scholars at the free school. Government was ready to aid it as far as was within its reach, and visitors to the Temple and residents, of all religion, in the town gave it their support. H. E. Sir Henry Blake and Lady Blake, to show their practical sympathy with the laudable work, visited it often; and today the school is as large as the funds will permit.

Lady Blake herself opened the Free Girls' School, housed in the building just outside the Temple gate. The education here is elementary; but with the book learning the little girls are getting a very practical training, so that in course of time they will be good mothers and housewives. Needlework is most carefully taught, and the little ones are trained to cut out and work for themselves. A kitchen is also in contemplation, where the pupils will be taught to cook.

The work of this School, as indeed of all schools of the kind, is of paramount importance to Buddhism as a religion. It ensures the growth of intelligent Buddhist men and women of the future, and the decadence of an intelligent appreciation of the tenets of Buddhism is largely due to the neglect of the tuition of the mothers when those mothers were little girls. The Girls' School is a very small and unpretentious building; but it is a work in the right direction, and worthy of all the support which can be given it, and worthy too of all imitation by Buddhists all the land over.

THE MAZE.

Standing in front of the *Dharmasala*, between it and the gate, is the labyrinth, or maze. It is the only one of the kind in Ceylon, and is meant to illustrate the difficulties of those lost in the round of births and deaths, with the persistent trail of sorrow and pain, which is the universal law of evolution and dissolution. The maze presents those bewildered persons searching, with keenness, but with utterly helplessness, for the cessation from repeated births and deaths. A group of life-size models at the end of the passage illustrates the pathetic scene in the last-but-one birth of the Blessed One. The *Bodisattva*, born as Vesantara Raja, perfected his qualifications for Buddhahood in charity by giving up crown and country, and at last giving his very wife and children.

THE BO TREE.

The bo tree is, of course, the sacred tree of the Buddhists It is under that tree that the Buddha attained to Buddhahood. The identical tree was at Buddha Gaya, Benares, India; and a relic of it is to be found in the Sacred Museum at Kotahena.

A branch of the sacred bo-tree at Buddha-Gaya under which Buddha became enlightened was brought to Ceylon 2400 years ago by Sangha-Mitta, the Buddhist Lady Missionary, daughter of the great Emperor Asoka of India, and planted in the Mahamegha Gardens at Anuradhapura, around which the Maha Vihara was built and where it is still growing, the oldest historically known tree in the world.

A branch of this tree at Anuradhapura was brought to Colombo by the Prince Priest, and is planted, in a specially prepared spot, opposite the image house, at the Kotahena Temple. The planting was done with due solemnity and appropriate ceremonial, the planting being effected by a nephew of the King of Cambodia, on behalf of His Majesty then in the Island on his return from Paris, who through press of other engagements could not undertake the ceremony in person.

It is interesting to remember that the little plant at the Kotahena Temple is a "direct descendant" of the original sacred tree of Buddha-Gaya, and is in consequence of great antiquarian value. A second branch of the sacred tree at Anuradhapura ever cut was grafted by the Prince Priest and sent to Siam, and is said to be thriving well in the Royal temple grounds there.

APPENDIX I.

(Reprinted from "The Independent," Ceylon, 22nd March 1905.)

Address By The Prince Priest.

On the first visit of H. E. Sir Henry A. Blake G.C.M.G. Governor of Ceylon.

PRINCE PRIEST JINAWARAWANSE then said: Your Excellency, in all countries the gift of knowledge whether wordly or spiritual has ever been and is still regarded as the highest gift which one may confer on another. Charity has always been taught as the most imperative of all social duties "Charity" says the Buddha "is to the world what the linch-pin is to the chariot." Imparting knowledge is included in charity and has always been held as the highest act of charity. Until modern civilisation was introduced into the East from the West, such an institution as a modern school was unknown to Oriental countries.

BARTERING KNOWLEDGE FOR MONEY

was never dreamt of. Education was never paid for. Whoever was qualified by a life-long preparation to impart knowledge, gave it freely. The only requisite for a pupil was earnestness of which he was required to give proof. One reads sometimes in ancient Oriental literature of large sums, as much as 1000 pieces of gold having being offered by a pupil to his teacher at his initiation. They were sometimes received to test the earnestness of the student, but always returned to the pupil with an additional contribution by the teacher to enable the pupil to start life on the completion of his education. And education to the ancient meant a thorough, complete education. But a smattering of it was regarded (and rightly too from the examples of it which we see now-a-days) a most dangerous weapon a two-edged sword.

One may naturally ask, how was a teacher able to support himself, and even make a gift of money to his pupil when he himself received no fees? The answer is that it was the custom of the East for the rulers, the nobles and the rich of the land to

MAKE GIFTS TO THE PUBLIC TEACHERS

in order that they may confine themselves to learning and education, free from all physical labour for their subsistence. It was thought that those who conferred the highest gift by way of charity should not be stinted in the very necessaries of life. Hence when the order of our Sangha arose kings, princes, nobles and wealthy men vied with one another in building temples and endowing them generously as gifts to the order, the members of which were public teachers in every sense of the word. Temples were public schools in ancient times. In Siam, where a Buddhist King still rules, Buddhist temples are still the public vernacular schools, although the teaching in them has considerably degenerated into elementary education as regard secular studies. We have, however, ample evidence to prove that teaching at the temples whether Hindu or Buddhist, was not confined to mere religious or denominational education, but that literary and scientific teaching of the highest order was also imparted there. The enormous quantity of Oriental literature, which still survives, that seem to defy the efforts of modern scholars to penetrate and bring to light ancient Oriental learning and the numerous monumental remains of ancient engineering and architectural skill will amply testify to the truth of this assertion. Bearing these historical facts in mind I propose to restore to this country if patriotic and broad minded Ceylonese gentlemen, who can lay claim to being the heirs to the most ancient civilisation in the world will only lend me a helping hand an institution

WHICH THEIR ANCESTORS HAD FOUNDED

and maintained with conspicuous success more than two thousand years ago, I mean Free Temple Education. In this scheme I also look forward to the time which, it is to be hoped, is not far distant when, under the new Buddhist Temporalities Ordinance, which has been introduced by Your Excellency, much of the temple revenue may be at the disposal of the public for the purpose of imparting free education in every temple that has revenue to spare. Should this scheme be successfully carried out education, I need hardly say, would receive much additional impetus and it will, in a considerable measure lighten the burden of tax-payers. Some people who have but narrow ideas of Buddhism and whose view of charity is limited to the Buddhists alone naturally object to secular temple schools and to education there being non-sectarian. This objection simply arises from the ignorance of the true spirit of the Master's teaching with regard to charity. Buddhist charity is universal, unlimited and all-embracing. It ***never begins at home*** but rather abroad if anything. The

MOTIVE UNDERLYING CHARITY

is "maitry" meaning friendliness or love. This maitry is a charitable thought that has no limit to its sway, it pervades the whole universe and applies to all sentient beings, and it begins first with those who need it most. Hence the diversity of the religions and nationalities of those who are interested in this truly charitablc undertaking is explained. We have here among the founders and supporters of this pioneer school which is intended to be an example to other temples to follow, Christians, Hindoos, and Buddhists as regards creed, an Englishman (perhaps I should say an Irishman), Tamils, Cambodians, Chinese, Sinhalese, Burmese and Siamese (labour only) as regards nationalities. It is a proof that we can, if we will stand on a common platform and labour in harmony for the common good. The power used to bring us together is indeed the greatest force known to man viz:- the power of love and truth. With the help of those interested in the welfare of Ceylonese children, men with whom wise and liberal views of education are a means to an end in the present life and not a speculàtion for the unknown future I entirely concur, I opened this

FIRST FREE AND NONSECTARIAN SCHCOL

for boys within these temple premises. All contributions by foreign visitors to the temple and to the sacred Musuem which, by the way, have increased three-fold within the space of 11 months since, I resumed duties as incumbent of this temple, I put entirely for the maintenance of this school. The arrangement is that founders and contributors are to support the school for a period of five months during which time it is hoped it will work its way into the favour and confidence of the general public and free the founders from further pecuniary responsibility.

The school was opened on the 5th December last with eight boys and the attendance increased gradually to upwards of 70, when 16 or more boys were taken away by force or false representation by an enemy of progress who in this instance has taken unfair advantage of the sacred robe which I wear.

Another project which should be mentioned here is the proposed opening of

A SISTER SCHOOL FOR GIRLS,

in the building which belongs to this Temple, which if carried out I am sure Her Excellency Lady Blake would have been pleased to manifest not a small interest, Mr. Oldham, one of the most enthusiastic and staunch supporters of this scheme of free Temple education is ready to open on his own efforts and responsibility with the help of his friends, and maintain the girls school for sometime. But unfortunately owing to the defect in the existing Buddhist Temporalities Ordinance the school building which we hoped to make use of for that purpose happens to remain in the hands of a private person who has been using it for several years as a private unregistered school in his own interest and although a letter of demand was sent to this person to deliver up the building to its legitimate owners, viz, the Temple authorities, he, to my regret, takes advantage of the resignation of the trustee of this Temple and refuses to comply with the demand. I mention this case because it is a good illustration of the unsatisfactory state of the Buddhist Temporalities Ordinance and I may add also the fact that that for nearly seven years that I have been connected with this temple every attempt at its improvement failed continually till I took the management of its temporal affairs into my own hand. Since then I

WAS ABLE TO INTRODUCE REFORM,

effect repairs and improvements and to turn this

Temple which had become a notorious place of refuge for undesirable characters into a respectable public institution which we now see.

In the interest of free and nonsectarian education in which everybody can help and in view of possible troubles that may arise in future and the necessity of providing means for overcoming such troubles under the circumstance which I have just briefly referred to, I would also suggest the formation of an association for the encouragement of

A REFORMED TEMPLE EDUCATION

by those interested in the scheme and that a manager be appointed to manage this school. The title of the association explains its aim and scope and I have but to explain the word "reformed" as meaning that education at Temples should be modified to suit modern progress and to meet both the requirement of modern life and nature and condition of the people and country and be eminently practical in its character giving an important place in its curriculum to agricultural and manual training, and that it should be treated as education pure and simple, secular and not religious and that it should be open to all creeds, sects and nationalities alike.

If this scheme should be successfully carried out the public will be benefited by many hundreds of ready-built school edifices, spacious and airy, I mean the existing preaching halls of Buddhist Temples which are only used for preaching once or twice a month and rarely, if ever, before 3 p. m., and many of the Up-country Temples with rich endowments are now used as barns or stores only.

With this somewhat long account of our work here for which I must apologise to Your Excellencies and at the same time confess my weakness in allowing myself to be overcome by the very great temptation with which Your Excellencies, informal visit to our school has brought, I, on behalf of those most interested in Free Temple education as well as my own,

TENDER OUR HEARTY THANKS

to you for your gracious presence here among us to-day, aud for the benevolent interest which you take in our welfare an interest which like the Buddhist *maitri* is all-embracing in its beneficence, and knows no distinction of creed, colour or race.

THE GOVERNOR'S REPLY.

H. E. the Governor:- Reverend Sir, I have listened with great interest to the views that you enunciated with reference to education in general, and especially your views as regards the possibility of spending any spare funds that may be found available for the educational progress of the people I need hardly tell you that you have my entire sympathy in any effort that you mav make to reach the people and to impart to them a sound and satisfactory practical education. I think every educationalist who helps in this great work is a real benefactor to the country and I wish your efforts in this direction every success in the future.

APPENDIX II.

(Reprinted from "the Morning Times" Ceylon, 17th August, 1906.)

———×———

THE SECRET OF CEYLON'S FUTURE WELFARE.

———

["*Times*" *Special.*]

We give below the interesting speech by the Siamese Prince Priest before H. E. Lady Blake at the opening of the Kotahena Girls' Free School. His remarks will repay perusal. They are his personal views, and are as fresh as they are honest.

Your Excellency, Ladies and Gentlemen:—In those happy times long gone by, when civilization, suited to the then stage of evolution of mankind, graced the East with her supremacy, charity was universal and pronounced by one of the greatest sages the world has ever known in these solemn words—

"Charity is to the world
What the linch-pin is to the chariot."

In other words a universal charity was proclaimed to be a necessity to the world; and the modern Buddhists have taken from the essence of the declaration a motto for Buddhist charity—

"Charity begins not at home."

To those noble and peaceful Arya people of old the world would have appeared upside down but for universal charity. A charitable spirit seemed to pervade the world of the East, for in practice life was regarded as sacred even to the meanest things that have lives. The helpless, poor and disabled, and the unfortunate dumb animals, could not exist to give them milk and honey without charity. This charitable spirit was extended even into the domain of religion, and religious controversy became popular, for it was carried on in the most amicable spirit with the most noble object—to the end that the highest truth may be found. All those good things have long been dead, which we Buddhists must ever bemoan.

A PERIOD OF UNREST AND STRUGGLE FOR EXISTENCE HAS COME

in obedience to the law of a zigzag course of evolution, to take the place of the peaceful *regime*, developing a civilization which began in the West and extends its influence to the East, giving birth to a new doctrine as its fruition, which the modern sage of a matter-of-fact world pronounces in these terrible words, "survival of the fittest?" We have the *zig* and now we are having the *zag* course of evolution. We can say with absolute truth that, could the noble Sermon on the Mount have a real hold on the heart and live in the daily life instead of in the mouth, of the West, this terrible doctrine could not have come to be recognized as a logical necessity for getting on in this world, and there would not have been an outcry of a "yellow peril," nor a sham "open door policy" where there is no strength to enforce it. to insult humanity. As a result, keen competition takes the place of peaceful co-operation for the common good, and the meaner among us, profitting by the admission of "the end justifies the means," do not hesitate to resort to wild tricks, and the hypocritical to tugging at the leg of friends, because this very spirit of rivalry for mere material gain.

RELIGION HAS BEOME A RECOGNIZED SORT

OF TRADE

and its administration a business, church-going a fashion and the *pansil* taking a profession, so that the noble doctrine of universal charity "charity is to the world what the linch-pin is to the chariot" has become, ***"you must greese the wheel*** with the oil vulgarly termed a "tip," or else a thick pair of boots and a long stick must be shown, in order to set the wheel of the chariot of present-day charity going. In this age of civilization of a go-ahead-quick, even the peace and quiet loving Buddhists must be astir, and they too must enter the field of competition if they do not want "to go to the wall." In short they must recognise the necessity of competition, though never will they forget the spirit of the all-compassionate Master's Teaching to be tolerant—a spirit which the West also teaches in the favourite quotation, "live and let live." To do this we are forced to recognize the first necessity of acquired knowledge and training as a weapon with which to enable men and women to fight the battle of life in the peaceful struggle for existence. All sorts of theories are brought forward to account for the degeneration of the world with the most frank acknowledgement that "we are degenerating," by those who hold this view. Among us the true natives of the East—I mean in the best sense fo being heirs to what our ancestors possessed of which we are very proud—we too have put forward our theories to account for alleged evils.

CONTACT WITH FOREIGNERS AND FOREIGN INFLUENCES

of all sorts being the favourite and most generally accepted. We claim that the plan of nature is that the universe will always be as it has ever been, a teeming variety and multiplicity, developing in harmony towards a common goal; and mankind is no exception to this law of Evolution and Dissolution progressing in a backward and forward fashion, epitomized by the life of a being from his conception to his death and the dissolution of the body into the four elements and *Vinnana-dhatu* which are capable of becomming one and *vice versa*. Had the world realized this doctrine, it would have "lived and let live'' in practice, and, perhaps no Anuradhapura riots to scandalize the late administration of this country. On the other hand those who hold the opposite view say that we ought to become all alike, one in appearance and feeling, each a *rose* and to *champaka*. The contempt expressed in the saying, "If you have seen one Chinaman, you have see them all," for the sake of simplicity and business facility, which the Civilisation of a go-ahead-quick world demands for its rapid progress, should be forgotten and become an expression of applause; and we should live as one man with one view and speak the same language which, in Ceylon, *should be English.* As a remedy for this deplorable state of things each camp puts forward all sorts of schemes for educating the people to their view of life, with the common recognition that knowledge is a first necessity, and they formulate various schemes with the result that schools of all descriptions and imperfections spring up like mushrooms with teachers most of whom have as much idea of education as a man in the moon and taken as much interest in their pupils' welfare as a clerk does in driving his quill, and who somehow can live on six pence a day with a family. All sorts of ends are to be attained by this or that scheme—some proclaim them honestly while others only as a policy for the attainment of some concealed ends—and each thinks that he has education in Ceylon. Lastly, though not of the least significance, this struggle for existence in Lanka has given birth to the Social Reform Society as a protest to the undue and indiscreet Western influenc of a low order, such as 'fashion' for instance. The fact cannot, however, be disputed that

WESTERN CIVILIZATION AND EUROPEAN INFLUENCE

have in general brought about the present state of things, which some hold to be good, leading towards the goal of *one-manness*, and others to be evil. Europeans *themselves*, however, justly claim to have done this, of which they have reason to be proud, and *they* are undoubtedly *responsible* for it. Only the other day at a discussion on Sinhalese arts the claim of Dutch and Portuguese influence was made by one of the speakers. The fact is that not only has there been Dutch and Portugese influence on Sinhalese arts; not only on arts alone have they left a mark of influence to be deplored by the natives, but the influence of the people of the West, now re-present by the English (in this country), not only on arts alone but on the very life of the people has become altogether *too much*; and the balance of harmony and unity in variety has been violently disturbed, which influence justifies the existence of the Social Reform Society, and even, within certain limits, the Swadeshi movement in India as counter movement against the aims of those of the opposite view of life, moulding the future to *a world of monotony*. It is vain, however, to say which is right but which ever is right, it in accordance with the scheme of nature, that will survive and flourish, and time alone can show which. The truth is probably to be found between the two extreme views, for it seems to harmonise with the law of nature. It is easy to see that it is so when one looks at the example which Japan sets before the world in being

EUROPEAN ABROAD WHILE REMAINING STRICTLY JAPANESE AT HOME,

and they are successful. Because they succeeded in destroying a hundred-thousand Europeans in a contest with European methods and weapons, but with a *home moral* born of a *peculiar* precept and training *unknown to the West,* they are accordingly recognized as a civilized and great people and are honoured with admission into the council of nations which alone are *to live individual lives.* But whatever be the truth, this much is certain, a civilization which sanctions wholesale application of the word *policy* and *diplomacy* as necessay practice in daily life—as effective and legitimate weapons with which to fight the modern battle of life in peace and war and worst of all the indiscreet application of the word "fashion" which turns intelligent beings into mere sheep, blindly following their leaders—I say the application of these words in daily life, if continued unabated, can bring but evil results in the end, for they *imply* a sanction of the questionable doctrine of "the end justifies the means." If in this age of go-ahead-quick the necessity for competition is admitted to be the right view, I too, even as a Buddhist monk, have a claim to a hearing among my fellows, of my theory and view of life, and perhaps a vanity when viewed from others' standpoint with spectacles peculiar to their creeds and those who say all priests are *une quantie negligeable*—and those wholesale extremists who say "all priests ought to *be hanged* for their *priest craftiness* and *greediness.*" I say to my fellows "give up the vain hope of a successful competition in the education of boys with those who have the command of *unlimited* means, but pay *great* attention to the education of your girls; for *every* girl you convert to your view and ways, you are making a profit in the conversion of a future *family*. Do not aim at making ladies and gentlemen of your students, but industrious men and women who should know what is good for them and what is good for only the *not-them*. Attend to the middle and the lower classes,—in fact the poor— who are

THE BACKBONE AND SINEWS OF THE NATION.

Begin education at home, *in the nursery*, in which character is formed, by educating the future mothers into capable teachers and let them complete their education at school. Aim at home life and comfort and industrious habits that they may get rice and curry, and *not* bread and butter, that they may *not* have to resort to *questionable* means of livelihood.

Make the girls understand that the mission ofa mother is *sacred* and of *very* great responsibility." I say much the same to the Social Reform Society. "Reform girls and boys, especially girls, and not men and women, specially the crusty old. Begin it at well-conducted girls' schools; and let the grown-up pupils, who have become eligible for marriage—who will be wives and mothers—be reformers for society *in the nursery at home,* and you *will* before long have a new type of men and women moulded by the irresistibly gentle power of woman's hands, and the *desired* regeneration will *then* begin." If girls could but be made to realise that the world lies at their feet and use rightly the irresistible power which nature entrusts to them and will neither abuse nor misuse it, a new world could be made by them, and a good world too, made by gentle *devi* and not savage *deva* as the present world was made." I often say to my Buddhist friends "attend to your girls and educate them to know the *possibilities* that lie *latent* in them, and the great responsibilities nature entrusted to them, and do not trouble yourselves about the boys who will soon be *captured* and *reformed* by the irresistible power of *well-educated* pupils of yours. But beware of the terrible consequences of dealing with such a *dangerous* power. For what chance has a poor man captivated by a charming

WOMAN OF CULTURE AND VARIED ACCOMPLISHMENTS

to *escape* being influenced and *led* by her? Only let women abstain from church-going and temple-worship, and both churches and temples *will* become empty on the most sacred days! The noble and gentle nature of a true woman is, however, a *gurantee* against the *injudicious* use of her power." At this view of life some laugh aloud, others in their sleeves and turn up their noses; some, while pretending to agree with me, set quietly to work to turn back the hand of my clock, and I am not surprised—for hypocrisy is terribly *common*—but a few others, however, honestly agree with me. I have, however, the satisfaction of receiving the encouragement of one whose opinion is likely to be respected by most of us in his brief remarks when I told him of my view: *"you know the world well—I quite agree with you!"* As a result those who agree with me have helped me by forming themselves into a committee to make arrangements for to-day's function to embark on a *venture,* according to the conception of life which I put forward, for the inauguration as announced of a charitable institution for *poor girls* as a sister school to the existing free school for boys, opened and working fairly well for now nearly two years, with the object explained in my address to His Excellency the Governor on his first visit to the Temple to which the school belongs. To this committee the thanks of all interested are due for to-day's arrangements or misarrangment. The scheme is to give *free education* to girls whose parents *cannot* afford to pay school fees, and, therefore, are those who have the *most* claims on *us all;* and on account of these being a great majority, they will form *the better half* of the sinews and backbone of the state.

OUR OBJECT

is to provide for a *natural* education which *begins with laying the foundation* of noble qualities and moulding of character *at home, in the nursery, by the mother* who alone can teach tender ones with enduring effects by educating girls to the standard of an *ideal* mother in this well-directed school, who shall be fit to fulfil the responsible and sublime duty of bringing up the young, who shall grow up to be honest and good citizens to their dearly beloved Lanka which exalted duty *nature entrusts to them*. In doing this we shall pay special attention to train the girls in *industrial habits,* and in giving applied knowledge needed for their station in life and *not* to make *vain ladies* of them. Home duty and home management which make home so dear and happy to a true English woman, and the *management of the nursery,* shall be cultivated along with simple and useful industry such as cooking, needle-work and kitchen gardening. An effort shall be made to show *moral essence,* in all their doings, in their daily lives, *without* the aid of the *figment* of a particular dogma or creed, for the school is mainly supported at present by non-Buddhists and must be worked strictly as a non-sectarian institution. The school will be under the control of the committee by which the boys' free school is managed. A most liberal-minded gentleman of the foremost rank among the communities of Ceylon in regard to culture and other distinguished attainments has come forward to relieve the committee of financial responsibilities by offering to take the management into his hand, and to find the necessary funds for working the school as a simple vernacular school for one ear, for which the public is much indebted, and the Ceylon Spinning and Weaving Mills ought to be proud. To carry out the *full* programme as explained *much more* funds than have been provided for are needed, and we shall endeavour to find them *from to-day* by appealing for support from the general public. This is the gist of our scheme. If what I have said in this rather long address, for which I crave your indulgence, cannot be expected to find general acceptance, I am certain that all will agree with me that the presence of Her Excellency in the chair is

[AN OMEN PROGNOSTICATING A FAR-REACHING SUCCESS

of this undertaking, justifying our hope and our aspiration for gaining the sympathy and support of the general public which the object aimed at and the name of charity which claims on us all justifies.

You will all agree with me also that the spirit of true charity and charitableness have been shown by the example of Her Excellency and those here present. She requires no artificial welcome by a lavish display of arches or false appearances or noisy-press getting-up to justify her presence but certainly an undecorated heart to open out to welcome her that shall be fit to duly appreciate and reciprocate the noble and compassionate heart that beats in unison with the many helpless poor within that motherly-looking figure in the chair who so well fills the place by the side cf our *Rajavaruvu* who knows eqally well the duty and responsibility of a representative of our truly Chakkavatti Raja of an Empire of varied races, interests, creeds and *traditons*, over which the sun never sets, whose motto seems to be "a fair field to all, and no favour." I will conclude with some words of advice to

THE COMMITTEE.

"You can never be too careful in educating girls for you are dealing with the creation of a future world in which your descendants will have to live." The names of some prominent gentlemen on this committee should however give us relief from undue anxiety. I believe we are able to turn out girls deserving of the honour which Her Excellency Lady Blake confers on us by her presence here to-day. Finally I cannot do better to encourage the committee and those who have the courage to begin with a small beginning to look at the baby school on their laps with optimistic eyes than by quoting His Excellency the Governor's words of encouragement given to the St. John's Ambulance Association the other day, "we should hope that this small beginning is a seed from which a large tree will spring up, shooting its branches into all parts of the Island, and doing inestimable good." Only I would change "doing inestimable good" into "making a more rational, peaceful and happy world for our descendants, that is, *our very selves,* to live in." I beg to thank Your Excellency, Ladies and Gentlemen, for the kind attention, indulgence and patience with which you have honoured my remarks.

PANORAMIC VIEW OF THE KOTAHENA TEMPLE